About the Book

In our fast-moving, ever-changing world, leaders at every level face constant distractions and demands. Becoming less reactive and more intentional, focused, and strategic can be daunting. What overwhelmed leaders lack is a powerful quality that, with practice, anyone can develop: *mindfulness.*

In *Show Up as Your Best Self,* executive coach Cathy Quartner Bailey presents a roadmap to becoming a more mindful leader. By applying the techniques she has shared with hundreds of Fortune 500 executives, you will learn how to cultivate a mindfulness practice to help you reach your leadership potential by being more confident, decisive, and grounded—even in the midst of chaos.

An expert on this growing trend, Cathy shows how mindfulness is a matter of carving out reflection time and leading with purpose. In a way that's clear and accessible, she explains how meditation and other forms of reflection can help any leader become more adept at:

* Managing uncertainty * Setting priorities * Listening actively * Solving problems * Developing and maintaining crucial relationships…and more.

Featuring illuminating leadership stories and interactive worksheets, this is a book for everyone striving to become a better leader while enjoying professional fulfillment and personal well-being.

Ten percent of royalties from *Show Up as Your Best Self* will be donated to Sheltered Yoga, a nonprofit organization that facilitates mental health and wellness through yoga and mindfulness education.

For more information about Cathy Quartner Bailey's executive coaching services, please visit www.quartner.com or contact her at cqb@quartner.com.

Show Up as Your Best Self

SHOW UP AS YOUR BEST SELF

MINDFUL LEADERS, MEDITATION, & MORE

Cathy Quartner Bailey with Zinnia Horne

Copyright © 2016 Cathy Quartner Bailey with Zinnia Horne
All rights reserved.

ISBN: 1523787198
ISBN 13: 9781523787197

To

Brad, Ari, and Gabrielle

*For family dinners filled with great food, stories, and laughter
and for giving my life purpose.*

CONTENTS

FOREWORD

Being able to *slow things down* is vital to being an effective leader. During my years as a leader in the airline industry, at British Airways, and other organizations, I found inspiration from great athletes, particularly when they were in the "zone." I marveled at how these competitors were able to collect the poise and confidence to almost effortlessly push through the most challenging situations. As my career progressed, I tried to slow things down so I could "show up" as my best self and make good decisions, particularly at critical times. Gradually, I learned that being in the "zone" was the result of taking time each day to quietly reflect, consider what I was doing, and think about how all the pieces fit together.

As an aspiring leader, I always tried to find ways to stay fresh and new while being true to myself. I made a commitment to learn from others, quietly reflect, and be deliberate about my actions. This stuff took time, especially because I wanted to be good at it. Not reacting to everything as urgent took practice. Sometimes I got it right and other times…well, I missed. Sometimes I was just too damn busy chopping wood to sharpen my axe. Sound familiar?

In today's world with a zillion distractions, it's too easy to lose sense of what really matters in life and find ourselves chasing down a rabbit hole after something that's just not that big of a deal. So now, perhaps more than ever, it's important for leaders to slow down and process what truly matters, taking proper time, attention, and care. When they do, results are so much better. And so is life.

Only after I retired did I come to appreciate the power of quiet reflection, prayer, and meditation as a way to clear the slate each day. Each night I take time to reflect and pray, focusing on the significant moments of the day with awareness and gratitude—helping me maintain my patience, purpose, and peace. Happily, both of my daughters—who are both busy mothers of four—do yoga regularly and love it because it helps them slow down and focus on what really matters.

Cathy's book is full of inspiring stories as well as practical meditation techniques, tools, and exercises to help today's leaders cultivate a mindfulness practice and "show up" as their best self. Someone once said to me, "In life you can have anything, but not everything... choose carefully." Choosing to embrace Cathy's guide to being an effective, genuine, and mindful leader is a great place to start.

Dale Moss has held several leadership positions in the airline industry, including CEO, OpenSkies; COO, Jet Airways India Ltd; chairman, British Airways Holidays; and director of sales worldwide, British Airways, where he led twelve thousand employees and was known for building great teams and delivering extraordinary results. He is currently president of Dale Moss Consulting Ltd.

You do not need to leave your room.

Remain sitting at your table and listen.

Do not even listen, simply wait.

Be quiet, still, and solitary.

The world will freely offer itself to you to be unmasked.

It has no choice.

It will roll in ecstasy at your feet.

—Franz Kafka

INTRODUCTION

We tend to overdo everything. Such conceptual actions just create more karma. Consider nondoing, nonaction, for a while, and leaving things as they are. This can provide balance.

—His Holiness the Twelfth Gyalwang Drupka

Are You a Human Doer or Human Being?

*Good leadership consists of
doing less and being more.*
—*THE TAO OF LEADERSHIP*, JOHN HEIDER

As a leadership coach, I partner with Fortune 500 executives. Again and again, my clients talk to me about waking up and feeling overwhelmed, running from meeting to meeting, and constantly reacting to shifting priorities, sudden mandates, and crises. While executives seek out coaching for various reasons, most of my clients want to get unstuck from their frantic, reactive routine to become a more strategic, more inspiring leader. They want to be a leader who excels at dealing with the many demands of a constantly changing, high-pressure work environment—while staying true to their mission and guiding their teams to achieve the best possible results for their business.

During the coaching engagement, executives figure out how to take time out, reflect, and prioritize. Gradually, they step away from the frantic "doing" mode toward a more strategic, balanced, and energizing "being" mode. Ultimately, they become more effective leaders.

Why "Show Up" as Your Best Self?

Think about a time when you were able to slow down and truly enjoy an experience or about a time when you were able to stay calm despite the whirlwind around you. Wouldn't it feel great to have that level of peace all the time?

Since you've picked up this book, you're probably interested in, if not already familiar with, the concepts of mindfulness and meditation. Exactly what does it mean to "show up" as your best self? Why does it matter? And how do you become a more mindful leader?

What Is a Mindful Leader?

A mindful leader is someone who brings out the best in one-self and others by consistently "showing up" present, grounded, and compassionate—especially in challenging situations.

To further break down that definition:

> *Leader:* someone who brings out the best in one-self and others
>
> *Showing up:* how you relate to yourself and others
>
> *Present:* in the moment, focused on the matter at hand

Grounded: the ability to maintain perspective, re-main calm, and stay objective

Compassionate: concern for others' well-being as well as your own

Challenging situations: any event that requires managing conflict or change and, in turn, cre-ates strong emotions and the potential for one to become stressed and/or triggered (fight, flight, or freeze mode)

Why Does Mindful Leadership Matter?

I'm stuck in this frantic mode, jumping from one task to another, not really accomplishing anything today. Where did the time go?

That statement of frustration reflects the daily re-ality of work for at least 80 percent of my executive clients.

We are all distracted. We live in a fast-moving, in-stant-gratification, tweeting, texting, and e-mailing world, making it hard to slow down, think about what matters, and "show up" with intention as our best selves. We often spend more time answering to our smart-phones than we do to ourselves. And as a result of con-stant demands from work, family, and community, we often find ourselves stressed out, emotionally drained, and physically exhausted.

Being a mindful leader has myriad benefits, personal and professional. Based on what my clients tell me, a mindful leader:

- maintains a clear, calm, and focused mind;

- "shows up" with more intention;

- sees the big picture and is less reactive;

- copes with difficult situations: effectively manages uncertainty, change, and conflict;

- listens better—more actively and deeply;

- sets priorities and focuses on what matters;

- brings a more creative and strategic approach to problem solving;

- excels at developing, repairing, and maintaining important relationships, which leads to more influence, greater impact, and better business results.

How to Become a More Mindful Leader: A Road Map

*We deal with our mind from morning
till evening, and it can be our best
friend or our worst enemy.*
—Matthieu Ricard

Yes, it's common sense. But it's not easy to practice. To effectively lead with intention, you need to take time out to reflect, prioritize, and focus. One of the best ways to become a more mindful leader is to establish a meditation practice. Among the many benefits, which I will discuss in more detail later, meditation will help you be more present to your current state of mind, which will enhance both your leadership ability and your well-being. The process of meditating includes focusing on your breath and/or setting an intention. In the beginning of each coaching engagement, I typically have to nudge clients to try meditation, having them start with just five minutes. My clients who are willing to try meditation notice the benefits immediately, often moving beyond that five-minute ritual and quickly expanding their daily meditation to between fifteen and twenty minutes.

The Meditation (or Journal Exercise)

There are different ways to carve out reflection time and lead with intention, one of which is meditation. In this book, I offer a four-step meditation guide and a worksheet to help you prepare for your meditation. While I encourage you to try the four-step meditation, it can also be used as a journal exercise.

What If Meditation Is Not for Me?

There is no right or wrong way to become more mindful and "show up" as your best self. The idea is to experiment with different practices that encourage reflection as part of your daily life. So if meditation is not your thing—or if you want to supplement your meditation—check out the "Beyond Meditation" and "More Tools" chapters of the book.

Learn from Real-Life Mindful Leaders

Rather than simply tell you how to become a more mindful leader, I'll let mindful leaders speak for themselves. In this book, you'll find inspirational stories written by everyday mindful leaders from wide-ranging professions and all walks of life. Many have influenced, coached, and mentored others to bring out their best, as well as shaped who I am. For successful leaders, including the ones I'll introduce, there is often a backstory of struggle, searching, and only then achievement. Hopefully, these leaders' stories will inspire you as much as they have me.

CHAPTER 1

WHY MEDITATE?

When we're in tune with our inner wealth—the qualities of compassion, contentment, patience, and so on—it's endless, it's timeless. Those are qualities that we're all born with. Everybody. The whole process of meditation is all about trying to dig into this inner wealth, to access it.

—TRINLEY THAYE DORJE

What Is a Mindful Leader?

A mindful leader isn't a natural-born charismatic leader. Anyone with the desire and dedication can become a mindful leader—that is, a leader who brings out the best in one's self and others by consistently "showing up" present, grounded, and compassionate—especially in challenging situations. One of the best ways to "show up" as a more mindful leader is to cultivate a daily meditation practice.

What Is Meditation?

Meditation is the practice of setting aside quiet time to calm our mind and relax our whole body by focusing on our breath and/or an intention. During meditation, we learn to let our thoughts flow, without analyzing them, obsessing over them, or striving to hold onto them.

So what does meditation have to do with being a more mindful leader?

The beauty of meditation is that it helps you unlock your potential to feel present, grounded, and compassionate from within rather than being dependent on outside stimuli. Meditation also enables you to gain more control over where you put your attention, instead of reacting to the moment.

While the term "mindfulness" has become somewhat trendy, meditating is an ancient ritual dating back five thousand years. Ancient people used meditation as a form of spiritual practice that enabled them to connect to their divine energy. In today's world where things move at the speed of light, connecting to your own energy can be as simple as sitting still in a quiet place for five minutes and focusing on your breath. In fact, numerous research studies have shown that a regular meditation practice will lead to a positive impact on the body.

The Mind-Body Connection

Routine stressors in the workplace—an abrasive e-mail, a contentious conversation, a high-stakes meeting—feel as real and as threatening to us today as a potential attack from a saber-tooth tiger did thousands of years ago. Whether it's a tiger or an angry colleague, we have basically the same physiological response—that is, we get triggered and stressed and go into fight or flight mode.

To better understand how meditation positively affects your physiology and helps manage your triggers, consider these scientific findings:

Brain—The amygdala, an almond-shaped structure in the brain, is responsible for handling our emotions. When we become triggered, we experience an "amygdala hijack." Blood literally leaves our brain and moves toward our limbs, so we can either fight or flee. This also negatively impacts our memory and cognitive function.

A regular meditation practice will improve your mental clarity and reduce the intensity and recovery time of stressful emotional triggers.

Heart—When we become triggered, the stress hormone cortisol is released, making us more susceptible to heart attack, stroke, and hypertension.

A regular meditation practice will help you manage stress and its harmful effects by reducing cortisol levels in the bloodstream. This leads to slowing your heart rate and lowering your blood pressure, helping you control your breathing and remaining calm.

Immune System—A strong immune system is critical to maintaining overall health. Antibodies, which fight bacteria and viruses, are critical to a strong immune system.

Meditation has been shown to boost activity in the areas of the brain that command the body's immune system, making it work more effectively. Studies have also shown that meditation boosts antibodies in the blood.

Based on my work with clients, the benefits of meditation include the following:

- A greater sense of self-awareness and awareness of the environment around you

- A calmer, more grounded presence

- Improved ability to regulate emotions, navigate difficult situations, and manage conflict

- Gains in creativity and innovative thinking

- Deeper active listening skills (being more present and patient)

- More compassion toward others and less critical of oneself

- Improved concentration and clarity of focus

- Enhanced perspective (the ability to see different sides and points of view)

- Stronger, richer, and more fulfilling relationships

If meditation is new to you, I encourage you to move out of your comfort zone and give it a try.

After meditating for twenty-plus years, I have found that the following meditation, "How to Quiet Your Mind in the Midst of Chaos,"* provides an excellent four-step

---

* This meditation is inspired by Rabbi Shapira (1932, Warsaw Ghetto) as interpreted by Rabbi Dr. James Jacobson-Maisels and adapted by Cathy Quartner Bailey.

structure. The flow of this meditation will enable you to get in touch with your breath and state of being, gain perspective, focus on what matters, and let go of what might be getting in your way.

You will find additional meditations listed in the "More Meditations" chapter of the book. All easy to grasp and practice, these meditations include one that can be done outdoors while taking a leisurely stroll; one that can be done sitting on a comfortable couch while sipping your morning coffee or tea; and one that taps into your inner glow—and will leave you feeling lighter. Give them a try!

CHAPTER 2

AN EXERCISE IN MEDITATION

If a person could observe the stream of his thought for only one day he would see that there is almost no distinction between himself and a madman. It is just that the madman actually acts upon his thoughts, but the thoughts themselves are indistinguishable.

—RABBI SHAPIRA (1932, WARSAW GHETTO)

Give Meditation a Chance

Becoming a mindful leader takes developing a sense of being in the present moment, staying calm and focused in the midst of chaos, and treating others with compassion. As a result, mindful leaders excel at bringing out the best in not only the people they're called to guide and inspire, but also in themselves. And one of the most effective ways to become a more mindful leader is to embrace the practice of meditation.

Meditation isn't something reserved for deeply spiritual and highly disciplined people. Meditation is a practical tool for gaining clarity of mind and feeling more relaxed and more confident. It's really that simple—and powerful. As I've stated, meditation requires setting aside quiet time (starting with as little as five minutes) to calm our mind by focusing on our breath or an intention. During the practice of meditation, we learn to observe our thoughts coming and going without clinging to them.

Tips to get started:

- Practice every day.

- Find a quiet place to sit where you will not be distracted.

- Establish a ritual. Meditate as soon as you wake up or at the same time each day.

- Try meditating for ten minutes total, focusing on each section for about two to three minutes.

- If you only have five minutes, just focus on section one. You can build out organically.

- Start small. If you are not able to do the entire four-step meditation process, just try step one: focus on your breath.

THE MEDITATION: "HOW TO QUIET YOUR MIND IN THE MIDST OF CHAOS"

ollowing is a simple, four-step meditation practice that I recommend to my clients and personally follow. In each step, you'll find examples to help you, but feel free to come up with your own. For more examples, refer to "More Tools" chapter: "Meditation Worksheet." For a full, guided meditation, visit my website, www.quartner.com.

Step One: Focus on Breath

Begin to notice your breathing.

> *Focus on your breath. Breathe in and say, "I am here." Then breathe out and say, "Here I am."*

> *Simply notice your thoughts coming and going without clinging to them. Visualize them floating away and then return to your breath.*

> *Refrain from any harsh judgment toward yourself.*

Once you become in touch with your breath, you are ready to move to step two.

Step Two: Have Gratitude

Think about and acknowledge who and what you are grateful for in your life.***

I am grateful for abundance.

I am grateful for good health.

Once you've spent some time reflecting on what you are grateful for, transition to step three.

Step Three: Set an Intention

Set your intention for the day—link to how you want to "show up" as your best self.***

"Show up" grounded and calm.

Slow down my pace, and listen to others.

Be compassionate toward myself.

Once you've spent some time reflecting on an intention, transition to step four.

*** *See the Meditation Worksheet in the "More Tools" chapter for more ideas, or come up with your own.*

Step Four: Let Go

Trust that your intention will happen without the need to force it on your end. Let things unfold naturally.***

Let go of harsh judgment toward myself.

Let go of thinking I need to be perfect.

Let go of worrying about things I have no control over.

Once you've completed the meditation, take a few minutes, and ask yourself the following:

1. How did I feel before I started the meditation? What was my state of mind?

2. How do I feel now?

3. What am I learning?

4. What might be some benefits from my meditation practice?

Remember to be kind to yourself.

- Recognize that it is normal for uncomfortable feelings to arise.

- Practice self-acceptance. Be kind, gentle, and nonjudgmental toward yourself. Whatever you experience is okay.

- In general (though some days will be more difficult than others), the more you meditate, the easier it gets.

- You can also use this structure as a journaling exercise.

You are enough, accept yourself.
—PEMA CHÖDRÖN

CHAPTER 3

BEYOND MEDITATION

If you can start the day without caffeine or pep pills,
If you can be cheerful, ignoring aches and pains,
If you can resist complaining and
boring people with your troubles,
If you can understand when loved ones
are too busy to give you time,
If you can overlook when people take
things out on you when, through no fault
of yours, something goes wrong,
If you can take criticism and
blame without resentment,
If you can face the world without lies and deceit,
If you can conquer tension without medical help,
If you can relax without liquor,
If you can sleep without the aid of drugs...

Then you are probably a dog.
—UNKNOWN AS INTERPRETED BY TARA BRACH

Want to complement your meditation? Here are other tips that will help you cultivate a daily mindfulness practice and "show up" as a more mindful leader.

Journal: Write down how you want to "show up" for the day. Write it down on a note card, put it in your pocket, and periodically check in with yourself, "How am I doing?" At the end of the day, journal about how your day went.

Prepare: Take a few minutes to prepare yourself for an upcoming meeting. This will help you be more proactive (versus reactive) in how you engage. By simply preparing for a potential conversation, you will be able to remain more grounded and calm. Plus, as one of my clients shared, you might even get a good night's sleep the night before a challenging situation. (See "More Tools" chapter: "Preparing for Difficult Situations").

Choose learning and curiosity over judging: This will help keep your emotions, body language, energy level, and mind-set positive, enabling you to "show up" in a more thoughtful versus reactive mode.

Take the balcony view: Be a third-party observer in your own conversation. That way, you'll be able to have a bit of distance and remain grounded and calm.

Get grounded: Feel your feet on the floor, breathe, and count to three.

Hit the pause button: Avoid blurting out the first thing that comes into your mind. Instead, take a moment to breathe and think about your response.

Stop multitasking: Think you're doing a good job at juggling everything? You're only kidding yourself if you think you're doing a good job at *anything*, if you aren't giving it your full attention.

Center yourself several times a day: As you jump from meeting to meeting in the course of a day, periodically remind yourself to take a deep breath and focus on the present moment. You'll become more centered and less distracted.

Get physical: Jog, walk, swim, kayak, dance, or try yoga. Find some form of enjoyable, energizing exercise that enables you to clear your head and get perspective.

Renew on a daily basis: Activate your parasympathetic nervous system, also called the renewal system, by engaging in energy-replenishing activities, such as listening to music, painting, reading, praying, or spending time with friends and family. Establish a consistent daily routine. Don't wait until you're burnt out; it's tough to binge renew.

Get a good night's sleep: Sleep reduces stress, restores brain function, and is important to self-control, memory, attention, learning, and problem solving. Going to bed a bit earlier is one of the fastest ways to reenergize in the midst of a long and stressful work week.

Power off your cell phone before and after bedtime: Give yourself the gift of time off from answering to other people by turning off your PDA for a set period of time before bed—and in bed—as well as on the weekends. If you can't turn your phone off for an extended period, at least find small blocks of time where you can choose to go offline.

Appreciate what you have: Keeping track of what you're happy and grateful for will help you maintain better perspective, boost your mood, and lower your levels of the stress hormone cortisol. This is also an excellent practice to do before bed. (See "More Tools" chapter: "Gratitude Journal")

Do a small good deed: Whether you help an elderly person cross a busy street or hold the elevator door for a frazzled coworker, you will remember what it feels like to be the kind and considerate person you are when you're not in a hurry.

Cut back on coffee: Caffeine is a powerful drug that triggers the release of adrenaline. Increased levels of adrenaline lead to stress and anxiety because they spur a fight-or-flight response. It's hard to make a decision and "show up" rational (versus reactive) when the blood has left your brain.

Take a break: If you lose your objectivity or become triggered, ask to take a five-minute coffee (decaf!) or bathroom break. Use it to center yourself by reminding yourself of how you want to "show up".

CHAPTER 4

MINDFUL LEADERS WHO INSPIRE: THEIR STORIES

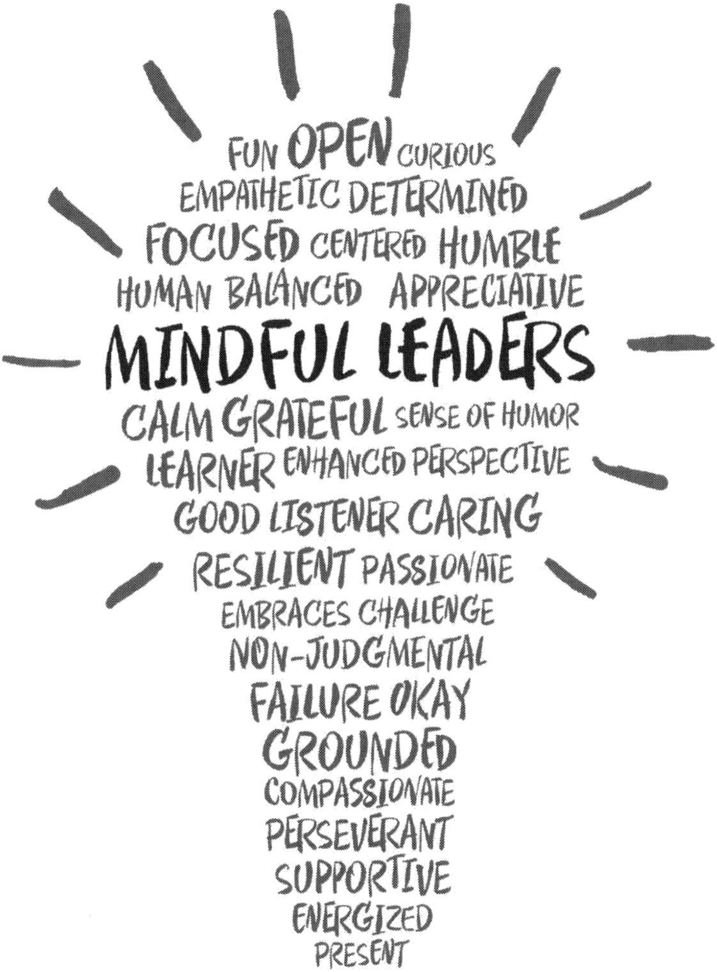
FUN OPEN CURIOUS
EMPATHETIC DETERMINED
FOCUSED CENTERED HUMBLE
HUMAN BALANCED APPRECIATIVE
MINDFUL LEADERS
CALM GRATEFUL SENSE OF HUMOR
LEARNER ENHANCED PERSPECTIVE
GOOD LISTENER CARING
RESILIENT PASSIONATE
EMBRACES CHALLENGE
NON-JUDGMENTAL
FAILURE OKAY
GROUNDED
COMPASSIONATE
PERSEVERANT
SUPPORTIVE
ENERGIZED
PRESENT

Do You Care? Leadership Lessons from Brother Bernadine, Archie Demarco, and My Dad

By Dale Moss

> *People don't care how much you know*
> *until they know how much you care.*
> —THEODORE ROOSEVELT

There are many things that make up a great leader, but to me, there is a common strand that binds great leaders together. It's *caring.* I have seen pyramids, trees, and all sorts of diagrams that overcomplicate what good leadership looks like. Of course, character, commitment, confidence, and competence are all essential qualities. But without caring, they are sterile.

Throughout my career, I have always tried to embody this critical element of leadership. The times I have demonstrated a sense of empathy and caring for the teams I have had the privilege to lead were the moments I felt most successful.

I have chosen to reflect on the people in my life who, by action, showed me what caring and leadership were really about and, in the most profound way, set the stage for my leadership style.

Brother Bernadine

I grew up on Long Island and attended St. Anthony's, a Franciscan high school. The school was located in Smithtown with an enrollment of only three hundred students. Brother Bernadine, our principal, personally greeted every single student by name as they got off the bus! Regardless of the weather, he stood outside in his cape, rain or shine, hot or cold, and greeted us, each and every day. He knew each student's name and how we were doing. Brother Bernadine was an impressive man who cared about his students, and we knew it.

One particular memory stands out in my mind. One day, Brother Bernadine pulled me aside and mentioned that my mom had not sent in my monthly tuition. He casually told me, "Tell your mom there is no need to worry, just send it in next month."

What I learned about leadership from Brother Bernadine was that he was loved and respected not only for being the principal, but also for being a *caring* man. He led from the front; as a result, his students would have gone through a brick wall for him.

We were a family with a culture unlike any school my other friends attended. It was simple and a great formula: Brother Bernadine *cared*, he showed it, and we all knew it.

Coach Archie DeMarco

Archie DeMarco was the athletic director and varsity baseball coach at St. Anthony's. He was a retired naval officer and had also played for one of the Cincinnati farm teams before joining the Navy. Coach DeMarco was a great guy—clearly in charge, tough when he needed to be, and (almost) always with a smile on his face.

I loved baseball with all of my heart and played junior varsity as a freshman. So when the spring of my sophomore year arrived, I was excited to try out for the varsity team. While St. Anthony's was a small school, we still had a competitive baseball team. Every few days during tryouts, a list was posted in the locker room with the guys who were still on the team. As I made it through three or four cuts, I remained hopeful.

Coach DeMarco knew both baseball and young men. One afternoon, he came to my classroom and asked if he could have a few words with me. As we walked, he put his arm around me and said, "Kid, you need playing time, and while you could make the team, I think it's best if you stay with the junior varsity team and get playing time. There are juniors and seniors who will probably play ahead of you. I'm going to need you in the next two years, but you need more playing experience."

This was potentially a moment of huge disappointment for me. However, I wasn't terribly crushed because Coach DeMarco *cared* enough to come to me, explain the situation, and ask for my support. He certainly didn't have to do that, but he clearly cared, and I am forever grateful. He took the sting and embarrassment out of the situation and encouraged me to keep working. As it turned out, he really was a genius because his decision to keep me on the junior varsity team worked out for the best. In fact, Coach DeMarco helped secure me a baseball scholarship to Fordham University. I could go on and on about how that experience impacted my life.

My Dad

My dad is the toughest softhearted guy I have ever known. And it took me many years to see, appreciate, and understand this wonderful combination of seemingly opposite styles. He grew up during the Depression in a difficult family environment and joined the navy at sixteen years of age during World War II. When I was growing up, Dad scared the heck out of me because he looked tough and took discipline seriously. In fact, everyone thought Dad worked for the FBI. But underneath, he was a real softy.

Toward the end of my senior year in college, I was struggling to find a job. Having gone to several interviews without any success, I felt sorry for myself and started moping around the house. This went on for several weeks until Dad had had enough. I was sitting in our living room reading when Dad walked in, a big book under his arm. He sat next to me and said, "Son, I know you are having a tough time, and your mom and I feel for you. We are prepared to help out in any way we can. But if you're looking for sympathy, it's under *S*." He dropped a big dictionary on the coffee table and left the room. In one instance, he showed me two contrasting qualities: *deep caring* and *self-reliance*.

Closing

Throughout the years, I have discovered that we truly learn life's important lessons in situations like the ones I just shared. I have been blessed to have people in my life who have demonstrated *caring* in different situations, and it is their actions that have enabled me to achieve whatever successes I have enjoyed and to better lead. I look back in deep appreciation to these loving, kind, and confident people and to many others who took the time to *care.*

*I met Dale Moss when I worked under his leadership at British Airways. He was inspirational, a terrific storyteller, grateful, and always brought out the best in us. Dale **cared,** and because he cared, we were motivated to reach our potential and do what was best for the organization. When I left British Airways, Dale told me I would always be welcomed back, and he continued to mentor and support me throughout my career.*

Dale Moss has held several leadership positions in the airline industry, including CEO, OpenSkies; COO, Jet Airways India Ltd; chairman, British Airways Holidays; and director of sales worldwide, British Airways, where he led twelve thousand employees and was known for building great teams and delivering extraordinary results. He is currently president of Dale Moss Consulting Ltd.

On a personal note, Dale has been married to Kathi Moss for forty-one years and has five grown children and ten beautiful grandchildren. "There is no question," Dale stresses. "My life's most important work is my family. I have been blessed beyond my wildest dreams and remain forever grateful."

Do You Know Your Best Self?

By Stephen Parker

Dan Cable, professor of organizational behaviour at the London Business School, says we are our best selves when we are doing *what we love, what people value, and what we're great at.* Yet our busy lives rarely bring us to this soul-sustaining juncture. Even the most successful professionals can feel trapped by what they are doing. They may be highly respected and richly reward-ed, but something is missing. Deep down, they sense that their work does not fully invite them to be their best self.

Some organizations get along fine operating this way, but when an organization is highly aspirational, helping people to be their best selves is imperative. I work in a highly aspirational organization. In 2013, we committed to a vision of A. T. Kearney being the most admired global full-service management con-sulting firm by the year 2020, while doubling in size. With those goals in mind, we built our learning efforts around this core tenet: for us to be the most admired firm, each one of us must be the most admired version of ourselves—our best self. This confluence of organi-zational and individual aspirations compels us to offer learning experiences that benefit the whole person, en-compassing the emotional, intellectual, relational, and physical domains.

Accordingly, our Expanding Horizons learning initiative (designed and delivered in collaboration with London Business School) takes a straightforward approach to helping our firm partners connect with their best self. We ask each participating partner to identify up to twenty people who know them well, be they colleagues, clients, friends, relatives, former teachers, and so forth. We then invite these individuals to share stories of when they saw the partner at his or her best. These recollections are submitted via a confidential web-based portal and collected into small booklets, to be shared solely with the partner being described.

Before we hand the booklets to the partners, we ask them, "What do you expect to see, in terms of themes and trends, in the stories about you?" This is a prompt to contemplate the best in themselves, which, for most, may be a refreshing respite from a lifetime of "constructive" self-critique. We then send the partners off to read about their best selves in a setting of quiet solitude, such as the gardens at London Business School. As you might imagine, reading these deeply personal recollections of siblings, former athletic coaches, teachers, past and current colleagues, clients and friends can be quite emotional. Partners often remark, "I had no clue they saw this in me." Those who invited only a few people to share recollections of them often wish they had asked for more.

The insights can be powerfully enlightening. For example, partners who believed that their best self is brilliantly analytical and results driven—based on the praise they have long received for achievements like being the fastest to earn an MBA or the first among their peers to be named a partner—may find that such strengths are not mentioned at all in their best-self stories. Instead, people who know them well recall instances when the partner was unusually caring and compassionate, startlingly generous, or steadfast in the face of crisis. This doesn't necessarily mean that the partner's previous sense of self is false, but rather, that it may be woefully incomplete. Such realizations create space for further growth by inviting our firm partners to bring more of their best selves to all they do and to help the people they lead be their best selves.

"It is easy for busy people to default to brief and transactional interactions," notes David Hanfland, an A. T. Kearney partner. "Expanding Horizons helped me to recognize that when I have really made a difference in people's lives is when I have slowed down to better understand what is happening with them and what I can do to help. I have a long way to go, but I am working on this every day. I can already see the impact it is having with my clients, colleagues, and family."

In an organization as aspirational as ours, the significance of being our best selves cannot be overstated.

There is simply no greater source of sustained commitment and zeal for achievement. The author Joseph Campbell once urged readers to "follow your bliss," but later suggested they would do better to "follow your blisters." For when we are doing what we love, what people value, and what we're great at, we give it our all. We then find great joy in our blisters. Ask yourself the following:

- Is your work life too often soul-depleting rather than soul-sustaining?

- How well do you know your "best self"?

- Are you willing to learn about your best self from those who know you well?

Stephen Parker is the first chief learning officer and global head of talent management with the consulting firm A. T. Kearney, where he applies his deep experience as a leadership consultant and executive coach to help his colleagues worldwide discover and apply the very best of themselves. Stephen, recently profiled in Chief Learning Officer, *has advised CEOs across many industries, including pharmaceutical, technology, and consumer goods, and has designed and led multi-year leadership and culture projects for global corporations. He previously served as president of a boutique leadership consulting firm in Washington, DC, and founded the global consulting group for BlessingWhite, an international leadership development firm. Stephen is based in New York City and lives in Princeton, New Jersey.*

Can You Remain Calm in Crisis?

By Dr. Joseph Zarge

> *The only thing we have to fear is fear itself.*
> —FRANKLIN DELANO ROOSEVELT

Like many adolescent science fiction enthusiasts of the 1970s, I read Frank Herbert's *Dune* and closely identified with the protagonist, Paul. When faced with a life-threatening situation, Paul would repeat this mantra to calm his mind:

> I must not fear. Fear is the mind-killer. Fear is the little-death that brings total obliteration. I will face my fear. I will permit it to pass over me and through me. And when it has gone past I will turn the inner eye to see its path. Where the fear has gone there will be nothing. Only I will remain…

Paul's words have stayed with me throughout my life, especially during challenging situations like my medical training, work as a physician, and athletic endeavors. In these moments, I have learned to focus on calming my mind so I perform to my best potential. Through experience, I know that once panic and fear take over, the likelihood of a good outcome drops considerably.

During my surgical residency in a trauma bay, I saw firsthand how the skill of remaining calm and not allowing fear or panic to take over is paramount. I quickly learned that while academic prowess and surgical skills were important, the residents who excelled were the ones who were able to perform under intense pressure and keep their cool—especially when blood is spurting to the ceiling from a patient on the verge of death. In these types of emergency, life-or-death situations, the medical leader who was able to remain calm made it easier for the medical team to follow instructions and achieve the best results for their patients.

There is a saying: "The first blood pressure to be taken in a life-threatening trauma code should be the trauma leader's and not the patient's. Calm yourself, then spring into action." My experience of being in the trauma bay reinforced the "fear is a mind-killer" mantra. By observing surgical faculty and senior residents, I learned the value of having a calm leader in charge—someone who did not get pulled into the fear or panic that present during a "storm" of trauma.

I chose vascular surgery as my medical specialty and trained in Chicago. I also had the good fortune to train under a chief vascular surgeon who was known for intraoperative tirades and giving residents a hard time.

However, I elected to choose him as my mentor because he had a reputation for being the best in the business. In the early days of my training, I remember being intimidated by this doctor's style—that is, his abrasive demeanor and verbal assaults during surgery. In fact, he would remain confrontational during the most difficult and delicate parts of the operation. Over time, I learned he had served as a surgeon in the military, operating in the most stressful environments. Eventually, I understood he was creating an exaggerated stress to see if I could perform under "wartime" situations. I realized he knew he would not always be there to assist me and was forcing me to develop the skill of keeping a clear mind during the most intense, extreme surgical situations.

To me, mindful leadership is the ability to keep one's mind clear and calm, especially during the most difficult moments. I've witnessed smart people make terrible decisions and mistakes, not because they did not know what to do, but because they were blinded by fear and panic. As a vascular surgeon in Atlanta, I continue to focus on remaining calm when there is a crisis, remembering my training and recalling the "fear is the mind-killer" mantra. In the operating room, I must lead and be certain of my decisions. It is one of the greatest rushes of surgery and also the most terrifying. Fear is the mind-killer, but remaining calm in life's storm allows the mind to see through the storm and beyond it.

Dr. Joseph Zarge is a successful vascular surgeon in Atlanta, Georgia. He is on the surgical faculty of Emory University School of Medicine and has been named as one of Atlanta's Top Doctors in Atlanta Magazine. *On a more personal note, one of Dr. Zarge's proudest accomplishments, along with his wife, Ellen, is raising two sons, one who was just named valedictorian of his high school. In addition to his professional work, Dr. Zarge relies on his "fear is a mind-killer" mantra during his many athletic endeavors, including skiing and tennis.*

What I Learned from Flipping Burgers and Scrubbing Pots: Lessons in Leadership

By Len Bardfeld

> *My religion is kindness.*
> —DALAI LAMA

I have had a range of job experiences throughout my life: minimum wage, work-study, entry level, and management. Each of these experiences influenced how I show up and what I value: hard work, collaboration, listening, and, most importantly, treating others with kindness and respect.

One of my first jobs was working in the kitchen of an overnight camp as "veggie boy." I made salads and prepped vegetables. I did this because in exchange for work, I could attend camp for free. I soon realized the kitchen was understaffed and that we would need to work long hours. Unfortunately, the manager did not seem to care about the team's morale, which sometimes made it tough for everyone to stay motivated. I learned that no matter how difficult a job might be, the importance of taking a deep breath, remaining calm, and completing it—despite my supervisor's attitude. I also made a promise to myself that I would care about the people I worked with and contribute to a positive morale.

In another fast-food job, I was in charge of cooking burgers and making fries. One of my teammates worked the register and struggled with math. Thankfully, we found a way to collaborate and support each other. When she needed help figuring out the change, she would yell out the numbers, and I would help her. And when the burgers were being ordered faster than I could cook, she would step in and help. This experience taught me that with collaboration not only are you able to get the job done, but the work is more fun.

In college at Cornell, I had a work-study job and found myself in the kitchen again. I worked a variety of jobs from short order cook to refilling beverage machines, but my favorite was washing pots, pans, and trays. Eggs don't wash off easily, so I decided to look at scrubbing trays as my workout. I would work myself into a sweat and entertain the others by making a lot of noise, banging tray, pots, and pans. The supervisors noticed how hard I worked and how well I got along with the team and recommended I apply to become a part-time supervisor, which I achieved. I learned that with the right attitude I could work hard, remain grounded, and inspire others.

Once I was promoted to supervise the Cornell kitchen, I focused on treating others with kindness and respect. One day a student was late. When he got there, he apologized. I sensed he expected me to chew him out, but instead I put myself in his shoes (I was also a student) and told him I understood. Had I not practiced compassion to this fellow student, our team would have been worse off—a disenfranchised worker and more work for everyone. This turned out to be a good lesson because he thanked me several times, always showed up on time, and did whatever it took to get the job done.

As I have transitioned into different leadership roles at Procter & Gamble, Dial, and Johnson & Johnson, I continue to practice what I learned from my earlier job experiences. However, I learned I would need new skills.

Because I had always worked in fast-paced environments, when I became a manager in the corporate world, I thought it was best to offer an opinion as soon as I had one. But that didn't work. In fact I received harsh but meaningful feedback to "shut up and listen" from my direct reports during a High Performance Team workshop. As I started to *really listen*, I built trust with my team, learned that solutions became richer, and found my team taking more ownership. That lesson was fifteen years ago, but to this day, I still remind myself to "shut-up and listen," as it's easy to drift back to old habits.

The importance of being kind, remaining calm, working hard, and listening are values I practice every day.

Len Bardfeld is a senior director at Johnson & Johnson Consumer Products Company, where he has worked for over eighteen years. He is well regarded and respected by his team— I often hear his colleagues and direct reports describe him as smart and fair, as well as an effective communicator. He is also known as a caring mentor, as he supports and provides valuable feedback to help others reach their potential and grow in their careers. In addition to being a seasoned professional, Len is a devoted husband and father. Len and his wife have three teenage sons and live in Yardley, Pennsylvania.

Ignoring the "Experts" and Succeeding with Balance

By Sonya Legg, PhD

> *Happiness is not a matter of intensity but*
> *of balance, order, rhythm, and harmony.*
> —THOMAS MERTON

When I started my freshman year at Oxford University, I was excited to major in physics and participate in many different extracurricular activities. However, I quickly learned that others, including my physics professor, had different ideas about how I should be spending my time as a college student. At the start of the year, my professor asked me what I did with my free time. I energetically replied that I enjoyed singing in the choir, rowing, running, and ballroom dancing. Little did I know that my professor and I had different ideas around the importance of maintaining balance and a sense of enrichment beyond academics.

Shortly after that conversation, I attended a meeting with my professor and dean and realized that, naively, I had overshared. The professor talked to the dean as if I weren't in the room, saying something like, "Sonya has a real attitude problem and needs to focus on her work. She is on the wrong path, and if she wants to succeed she is going to have to devote herself to physics, and only physics." He then turned to me and said, "So, Sonya, what do you have to say for yourself?" Having just graduated from a high school that encouraged students to develop through academics and extracurricular activities, I was in shock, feeling betrayed and disappointed. While I knew balance was important, I was caught off guard and unable to say anything.

I left the meeting feeling deflated and contemplated dropping out of Oxford. But, thankfully, that night a good friend encouraged me to continue, telling me "be who you are" (our high-school motto). In the end, that's what I did. It occurred to me that my supposed mentor, my physics professor, was quite narrow-minded. Fortunately, my first-term final exam results proved him wrong, and I excelled.

The most important lesson I learned during college was that if I did not take time to renew, I risked burning out and not feeling motivated enough to focus on academics. My four-year experience taught me that in order to be excited about science, I needed to take time to socialize, interact with others, and explore other activities. From then on, apart from my professional and academic interests, I made sure to enjoy activities like singing, running, and spending time with friends and family.

My professor formed an opinion of me based on whether I fit his idea of a scientist (that is, someone without outside interests, someone interested only in science) and not my actual performance. While I wanted a career as a scientist, I also imagined a balanced life that included a social life, non-science-oriented interests, and, eventually, a husband and family.

Despite my professor's best efforts (ha!), I rebelled against his idea of being a "true scientist," and I have not looked back. I'm still running, singing in a choir, and enjoying the fun activities that help me manage stress, gain perspective, and show up grounded and calm. Over the years, I have found that one of the best ways to solve a challenging scientific problem is to go for a run, clear my mind, and let things sort themselves out.

Now that I am an established professor and scientist, I have the opportunity to encourage students, both men and women, to take time out, explore, and lead balanced lives. I am also proud to say that my husband and I are raising two daughters who are not only thriving academically but also growing as well-rounded people as they explore the outdoors, play their musical instruments, and enjoy cultural activities.

Sonya Allayne Legg earned a PhD in dynamical meteorology and oceanography from Imperial College, UK, and a BA in physics with first class honors from Oxford University, UK. She currently works at Princeton University as the associate director of the Cooperative Institute for Climate Science and a Research Oceanographer in the program in atmospheric and oceanic sciences. Sonya is passionate about mentoring women scientists; is involved in PWiGs (Princeton Women in Geosciences) at Princeton University; and serves as a coleader of MPOWIR (Mentoring Physical Oceanography Women to Increase Retention), a nationwide mentoring program.

Sonya enjoys spending time with her husband and two daughters as well as gardening, singing, running, and traveling. Her most recent accomplishment includes training for and completing the Philadelphia marathon.

The Right Thing at the Wrong Time Is the Wrong Thing

By Joan Spindel

> *I learned that we can do anything, but we can't do everything…at least not at the same time. So think in terms of your priorities not in terms of what activities you do, but when you do them. Timing is everything.*
>
> —DAN MILLMAN

In my twenties, finding a job to pay the rent, learning, expanding my social network, and traveling the world were my only objectives. Timing in life is everything, and thankfully, it was the 1980s, during the technology boom. While I had no real work experience, hard workers were needed, and I successfully talked my way into and landed my first job.

In my thirties, I transitioned out of my individual-contributor role and started leading and managing teams. I was often the only woman leading a meeting or presenting at a conference; neither female role models nor mentors existed for me, but despite that, I did okay. I never really thought about "leaning in or leaning out." There were no fancy formulas; I worked hard, learned new skills, and delivered results. So while it wasn't part of any grand plan, I ended up working for organizations like EMC, Lotus, and IBM—early pioneers and innovators in the world of technology. In time, I became chief marketing officer for a sexy technology start-up. Life was good.

It was also during this time that I met my husband (another technology geek!), fell in love, got married, and decided to start a family. There was a sudden shift in my values—excelling at work seemed less important, and having a baby became my new focus. Unfortunately, it didn't go as planned: I learned I was not able to conceive. It was a difficult and painful time for me. But in the end, my husband and I decided to explore adoption. It turned out to be the best decision of our lives. We soon welcomed a beautiful baby boy into our family. It was love at first sight.

Ironically, when our son came home, I was also offered my dream job at a Fortune 500 company. It quickly became apparent that I wouldn't be able to honor my family values and be an executive at the same time. Despite really wanting the job, in the end I turned down the offer. I knew I needed flexibility and that that role was not where I would find what I needed.

After much internal debate, I decided to go it alone and set up my own tech-marketing consulting firm. It wasn't so easy to leave an exciting job with benefits, steady income, and fancy title that commanded respect. And given my introverted nature, I was not sure I had the chutzpah to make it on my own. But over time, my professional network and diverse work experience helped me land clients, and fortunately, my business grew.

In my new role as an independent consultant, I redefined personal and professional success. The ability to scale business up or down in order to meet my own personal needs became more important than titles, teams, and steady income. I have come to learn and truly appreciate that, while not always easy, honoring my own values versus allowing others to define what's important to me is what true success looks like.

My family life is rich, and my son is a flourishing teenager. Because I met life on my own terms, I have been able to be mindful about how I wanted to show up as a mother, wife, daughter, friend, and professional woman—and, ultimately, define and live my own definition of success.

Joan Spindel, general partner of the Scarsdale Group, has twenty-plus years of experience creating and developing marketing strategies and tactics for both high-technology and services-led companies. She provides consulting services to a variety of organizations, including Fortune 100 firms, start-ups, and nonprofits. She helps organizations launch new products/ventures ("Launch It") or solve problems ("Fix It"), often filling in as acting CMO for companies in transition.

In her spare time, Joan enjoys hosting parties, working out at the gym, painting, and spending time with her husband and son.

When Failure Is Not an Option

By Christopher Stevenson

> *I can accept failure, everyone fails at*
> *something. But I can't accept not trying.*
> —MICHAEL JORDAN

During my junior year of college, I became enamored with the sport of rowing and decided to give it a try. I signed up for the rowing club, attended practices, and set an ambitious goal of earning a seat on the "first boat"—that is, the top-tier rowers on the team—particularly challenging, given I was competing against others who had been rowing since freshman year or earlier.

I started training and continued to fall in love with the sport of rowing. Not only did my body become strong and lean, but I enjoyed the camaraderie of fellow rowers and the beautiful sunsets along the river. However, I was not yet aware of the true gift rowing would teach me.

In order to earn a spot on the first boat, we needed to pass a twenty-five-hundred-meter test. Because I was already a junior and a novice, I was nervous and fearful I would fail. My goal was to finish in sub 8:40 (8 minutes, 40 seconds).

After a considerable amount of physical training, it was now time to take the test. So, with butterflies in my stomach, I took a deep breath and started rowing. The first fifteen hundred meters were a breeze. I remember thinking, "Wow! I'm at a sub 8:30 pace—that's even better than my sub 8:40 goal!"

Unfortunately, things quickly changed. My heart was beating faster than I could take, and my legs were on fire. In other words, I was well past my pain threshold. My mind took over—and not in a good way. I could not mentally push through the pain and hang in there. And with just seven hundred meters to go, I began to slow down. I started gasping for air and could not complete the test. I have never forgotten the look of disappointment in Coach Bob's eyes or the feeling of being a complete failure.

Rowing was no longer just about sunsets and having a good time. I would have to change my focus in order to meet my goal. After spending several days moping around and contemplating quitting, I realized failure was not an option and decided to give it my all.

I shifted my focus from the physical to include mental preparation. I practiced rowing, but more importantly, how to calm my mind and manage through the physical discomfort. I visualized successfully achieving my goal. I was prepared for the next opportunity, mentally and physically, and earned a spot on the first boat.

This turned out to be one of the best experiences of my life. Not only did I learn a valuable lesson about resilience and mental preparation, but I also went on to have a rewarding, competitive rowing career during college and beyond. The challenges I faced during my college rowing years are not unlike the challenges I face today in the business world and raising two daughters.

As a team leader, my focus continues to be on how I mentally prepare myself and manage my own discomfort, in order to do what's best for our team and the business. Focusing on "how I show up," for others and myself, is as important as understanding the business issues. Taking time out each day to reflect and renew has made it possible for me to remain calm, centered, and manage through tough situations and decisions.

As the father of two daughters who focus on their academics, participate in competitive sports, music, and other extracurricular activities, I try to instill the value of meeting challenges head on and never giving up. I remind them that we often learn more from our failures than our successes and to ask the important questions:

1. How dedicated are we?

2. How resilient are we?

3. And, ultimately, how mentally prepared are we to face the tough moments, to remain calm and centered, and to achieve our goals?

Christopher Stevenson is a managing director for a reputable professional services firm, where he is responsible for advisory financial risk solutions, financial technology innovation, and cyber risk management for large financial services clients.

On a personal note, Chris is an avid athlete, still training in rowing (though sometimes in his garage!), biking, and hiking. He lives in New Jersey and enjoys spending time with his wife and two daughters.

A Lesson from McDonald's: Life Is an Occasion— Rise to It!

By Sang Lee

Great leaders don't set out to be a leader…they set out to make a difference. It's never about the role—always the goal.

Introducing My Dear Grandmother

I would like to share a personal story of the woman who raised and shaped me to be the person I am today. For most of my life, I thought she was my grandmother, but I later learned she was a close friend of my maternal birth grandmother's. So for the purpose of this essay, when I mention my "grandmother," I will be referring to the woman who raised me.

In 1971 when I was born, my mother had health issues and was not able to care for me. Consequently, I spent most of my childhood with my grandmother. She was my protector, defending me from my parents and two older siblings, regardless of how irrational my behavior was. To this day, I have fond memories of Grandmother sneaking me food when I refused to eat with the rest of the family.

My grandmother loved me unconditionally, but this is not the main point of the story. What was remarkable about her was that she was physically disabled. Unfortunately, when she was a child, she fell off a wagon and damaged her spine. As a result, she became a four-foot-tall woman with a severely curved spine, making her look like a hunchback. While her appearance did not bother her at home, it did in public. She rarely ventured outside.

When I was nine years old, my father was offered (and accepted) a job with the Korean Embassy in Washington, DC. Our entire family obtained visas to move with him, except for Grandmother, because she was not a "blood" relative. Upon hearing this, I screamed, cried, and carried on for days, driving my parents crazy until they somehow figured out a way to secure Grandmother a visa.

So even in the United States, Grandmother continued to care for my sister, brother, and me, cooking our meals and taking care of the house. She was the glue that kept our family going, the real COO, while Mother was more of a figurehead.

Life Lesson in a Single Impressionable Event: The Story of McDonald's

After living in the United States for about three years, my father was promoted to a new position located in

South Korea. The timing was not ideal because my older brother was about to leave for college. Because of this, my parents made the tough decision that they would move to South Korea and leave us with my grandmother and guardians. Our guardians were mostly there in case of emergency, and in reality, it was my tiny grandmother, who did not speak a word of English, who took care of my brother, sister, and me—on her own in a foreign country.

There is one event that stands out during this time that has had a huge impact on my personal and professional development. One day, my sister and grandmother went shopping. I was a huge fan of McDonald's chicken nuggets and asked my sister if she would stop by McDonald's to get me some. She replied that she was busy and that McDonald's was too far out of the way to pick up "junk food" for her little brother.

A couple of hours went by, and my sister returned home, alone. When I asked her where Grandmother was, she answered that Grandmother had insisted on going to McDonald's to get my food. I became furious at my sister for leaving Grandmother, a woman who hated being out in public and couldn't speak a word of English, to venture out on her own. My sister and I argued for what felt like an eternity until we became concerned that Grandmother might be lost. That's when the front door opened, and Grandmother walked in, holding a bag from McDonald's containing my chicken nuggets and favorite BBQ sauce! Relieved to see her, I shed tears of joy and gave her a huge hug.

Impact on My Life

To this day, my sister and I talk about the McDonald's story whenever we discuss the impact Grandmother had in shaping the person I am today. I always envision what it must have been like for the McDonald's employees to see this little hunchbacked Asian grandmother desperately attempting to get food for me, her grandchild. My grandmother, who for an instant, probably didn't care about the obvious stares she must have received due to her appearance and inability to speak English. She was determined to fulfill her mission of making me happy. The amazing thing about the McDonald's event was that when Grandmother returned home, she acted as if nothing special had happened.

I often think of my grandmother, a remarkable woman, who, even though she experienced doubt and fear, was still strong, humble, and compassionate enough to rise to meet any situation head on and make the most of it. She was a person filled with love and compassion, who demonstrated, through

repeated actions, the importance of humility and quiet confidence. These lessons have always stayed with
me. As a result, I try to guide and remind my family
and colleagues that it is okay to have flaws, weakness-
es, and fears, but despite these, we must rise to meet
the occasion.

My beloved grandmother is no longer physically
with me, but not one day goes by without me thinking
about her and appreciating her unconditional love for
me. And, most importantly, I try to live my life, both
personally and professionally, reflecting on the lessons
learned from my dear grandmother, who showed me
the true way to lead people is through love, compassion,
humility, and quiet confidence.

*Sang Lee is a managing partner at Aite Group, a research and
advisory firm to the top two hundred financial institutions,
leading technology vendors and professional services firms. I
met Sang when my husband, Brad, worked with him at Aite.
I am always inspired by Sang's humble, kind, and authentic
leadership style.*

*On a personal note, Sang is happily married with three chil-
dren and describes himself as "the worse half of a beautiful
relationship."*

*We Do Not Honor the Dead by Dying with Them…
In the Midst of Difficulty Lies Opportunity*

By Rick Gardner

One of the most profound experiences on mindful leadership I have known came out of a family tragedy. On September 26, 2007, my oldest son, Zia, died suddenly of a previously unknown and undetected heart condition. He was thirty-four years old. Zia was home alone in the early evening and had called 911. The apartment was a four-story structure, and he was on the third floor. Paramedics arrived but initially could not get in, since the door was locked. By the time they were able to break down the door and get to the third floor, Zia had died. I quickly called our son James to deliver the terrible news. James was living about ten minutes away from us at the time. I told him we would bring our youngest son, Jeremy, over while Diane and I made the trip into town to see Zia. My wife and I now belonged to a club that no one wants to join: surviving parents of children.

While we were fortunate to have abundant support from family and friends during this difficult period, I realized that everyone would need to deal with this loss in their own way. I had no idea what that would be even for myself, let alone for others.

So what did I do?

I slowed myself down.

I focused on helping others and doing the next right thing, even though I was not quite sure what that might be.

I allowed myself to grieve. Often, I was alone. Other times, my grief came out at random moments in the presence of others.

I gave everyone whatever space and time they needed to move forward. At times, it was just being present with them in the silence of the moment. Other times, it was doing even the smallest of things together in a thoughtful way.

So what did I learn?

I discovered I could function well, though certainly not perfectly, during moments of extreme challenge.

I was able to provide comfort and stability for others by focusing my attention on them and being attentive to their needs.

While struggling for meaning, I could still be grateful.

One thing I had not anticipated was how many people would feel awkward around me after Zia's death. They were unsure how to act, what was appropriate to say, or even what the best way to be sensitive was. I simply said to them, "We do not honor the dead by dying with them."

Indeed, it was devastating but not disabling. I said that I wanted to turn this family tragedy into a source of strength.

I told them I appreciated their compassion and explained it would be helpful for me to go back to doing what we had been doing before all of this happened. By stating my wishes, I was able to provide the acknowledgment and relief they needed to move forward, and it certainly helped me in establishing a new normal.

I continue to live in the *now* and am ever mindful of the fleeting moments of life.

I choose to create high-quality personal and professional experiences moment by moment for as many moments as I have left.

While I will forever grieve the loss of my son Zia, I have never felt more alive and grateful for the ability to serve others as a coach and consultant. I am able to help people deal with their own personal and professional leadership challenges by drawing on this profound experience.

I hope that by sharing this story, I can offer you a moment of thoughtful reflection and enable you to move positively and steadily forward on your own journey of becoming a more mindful leader.

I'd like to thank Rick for sharing his personal journey of how he lived through a family tragedy. I have had the privilege of partnering with Rick for many years, facilitating workshops in the area of conflict management. Rick always shows up grounded, positive, insightful, kind, and easily able to connect with clients.

Rick Gardner, president at GEMCAP Ventures, LLC, works as an executive coach and business consultant with teams and individuals.

Someone Throw Me a Life Jacket!

By Meryl Moritz

> *Alone we can do so little; together*
> *we can do so much.*
> —HELEN KELLER

My parents fed and housed me but did not provide much guidance. As I look back, one memory in particular stands out. I remember my father tossing me into a pool, and because I did not know how to swim, I sunk like a rock. I was frightened and angry when my father fished me out, laughing. I received the message loud and clear: figure it out myself and don't ask for help.

Fast-forward fifteen years. I'm now in my post college life and living pretty much on my own. The idea of asking for guidance was the furthest thought from my mind. I participated in the era of drugs, sex, and rock 'n' roll; spent time with people who were going nowhere; and married the wrong man. As a result of my choices, my self-esteem suffered. I knew I needed a change, but given my history of not asking for help, I did not know where to turn.

A friend who lived in my building suggested I attend a women-only in-career-transition workshop. I signed up, attended, and—for the first time—experienced women asking for help from each other. Throughout the twelve-week workshop, I researched different fields, reached out to my network, and, while it felt uncomfortable and a little anxiety provoking, asked for help from everyone I knew. The visual in my head of my father tossing me into the pool was still there, but now other women were throwing me a life jacket. I did not have to do it alone.

Soon after the workshop, I found a career that was a perfect fit for my talents and interests and landed a job in a large, reputable public relations firm. With my confidence growing, the domino effect went into play. Over the course of the next three years, I was promoted to VP, received multiple raises, and finished grad school with high honors. My increased sense of self and confidence spilled over into my personal life. I finally had the courage to leave a marriage that wasn't healthy and got remarried to a sentient, thinking, whole man. I wouldn't have been able to make these changes in my life had I not had the support and guidance of others.

As I look back on my experience as a seven-year-old, the "do it yourself" philosophy did not work for me: all it produced was a feeling of loneliness and an aversion to ask for help. Thankfully over time, I have learned it can take one courageous act of asking for help—whether during a Women in Transition Workshop, finding my first female mentor, or hiring a career coach to start a domino effect and get things moving in the right direction.

During the last decade, the foundation of my work and life passion has been supporting young women build meaningful careers, helping homeless women get back on their feet, and sponsoring women in war-torn countries obtain education in order to meet basic needs for themselves and their families. Often my mentees' accomplishments exceed my own. This delights me because I can pay it forward and throw a life jacket to someone else in need.

Meryl Moritz, principal of Meryl Moritz Resources, holds a special place in my heart. I met Meryl while she was teaching coaching at NYU and knew that she was someone I wanted to model my career after. She mentored me with her generous spirit and love of coaching, supporting me and even throwing me a life jacket the many times I found myself in over my head. I would not be where I am today without her.

In addition to being principal of Meryl Moritz Resources, she continues to help others in her roles of former vice chair of the International Coaching Federation, teaching at University of Miami, and coaching fellows through SupporTED.

How Would You Show Up with Six Months or Five Years Left to Live?

By Cathy Quartner Bailey

> *Be kind, for everyone you meet*
> *is fighting a hard battle.*
> —ANONYMOUS

"You have lung cancer and six months left to live," said my father's doctor. Fortunately, the doctor was 100 percent wrong. Dad did not have cancer but instead aspiration pneumonia and five more years.

But aspiration pneumonia, while not cancer, had its own set of difficult complications. Unfortunately, Dad had lost his ability to swallow properly because food and liquids were going down the wrong pipe, into his lungs, and causing infection. During his final five years of life, I watched this once invincible, active man, who used to refer to himself as "one handsome devil," fight for his life.

So while the disease took away my father's ability to eat, drink, and breathe on his own, it did not take away his ability to teach us how to live and how to love. For the remainder of his life, my dad was deprived of the simple pleasures we often take for granted; he used an oxygen machine and had a tracheotomy and a feeding tube. His medical charts had "NPO" stamped on them, acronym for *Nil Per Oz*, a Latin phrase that translates to *nothing through the mouth: no food and no water.*

I don't think anyone, including my dad, would have believed he could endure these new set of circumstances, but somehow he did—rising to the occasion and teaching us the meaning of really hanging in there and surviving.

Nine Lessons from My Dad

Always have a sense of humor

My dad had an incredible sense of humor, and thankfully, the illness did not change this. His arms were covered with bruises and scabs from the many needles administered, but rather than feel sorry for himself, he often joked about his predicament, calling himself a "human pin cushion." Up until the moment he died, he kept his sense of humor. In fact, right before he died, when his nurse asked him to open his mouth for morphine, Dad jokingly said, "I thought you were a nurse; since when did you become my dentist?"

Take care of yourself first

One day I went to visit Dad in the hospital. I rose early, barely brushed my teeth, and drove quickly to the hospital because I wanted to be there when he awoke. He opened his eyes, took one look at me, and said, "Go home; you look terrible." I learned I was no good showing up for someone if I wasn't taking care of myself.

Soon afterward, my dad was put in a medically induced coma so his lungs would benefit from something called a RotoProne. I walked into the ICU, and there was my father, unconscious and spinning around like a rotisserie chicken. I made sure I was at the hospital when he awoke, but this time, I put on my Chanel makeup, fixed my hair, and wore something nice. His doctors told us Dad might not be coherent, that his brain might have been damaged, and therefore, he might not be able to communicate with us. Thankfully when he awoke, not only was he coherent but also said, "Gee, you look wonderful; did you do something different with your hair?"

Keep perspective

I learned to take care of myself and find ways to take a step back and maintain perspective. I practiced yoga; took long walks; and kept in touch with family, friends, and colleagues who provided comfort and support. I kept on working because my clients and colleagues helped me to be in the world of the living (at a time when I was surrounded by so much dying) and stay centered and grounded.

How to listen

I learned that sometimes the best kind of listening is just being with someone and being quiet. On many occasions, I drove from New Jersey to Maryland just *to be* with my dad at the hospital. Not many words were exchanged, but we were connected.

Be grateful

I learned to be grateful for the simple pleasures of life. Taking a walk, breathing, eating, and drinking. A lick of a coconut popsicle, a sip of water—these were a few of the treats we would sneak for Dad when no one was looking. He often joked and laughed about what he would do for his favorite meal: a bacon cheeseburger, fries, and a coke.

I was also grateful for my husband and siblings. My husband, at sacrifice to our own immediate family, always encouraged me to visit my dad. And because of this, I have no regrets. My siblings and I took turns, juggling our schedules, so that we could support each other as well as my mother and father.

The so-called experts are not always right

My mother, who never attended college, understood my dad's illness better than many of his doctors and nurses. She intercepted unnecessary procedures and even a few surgeries (just before he was being wheeled away) by understanding his situation and being his advocate.

See beyond the physical

One Father's Day, I went to the hospital to give my dad a card. He started to cry. I had never seen him cry before, so I asked him, "What's the matter, Dad?" He told me he was embarrassed by his situation and sorry I had to see him that way. I don't remember what I said, but I do know I learned to look at my dad, see him for the man he was, beyond his physical condition and limitations—and not let his illness define or diminish him.

Listen to your own voice

I learned to trust myself and do the right thing. While well intentioned, I ignored comments like, "He's an old man; you have a young family. You're busy; he can do without a visit." The times I spent with my dad were gifts for both of us.

Be true to yourself and your own values

After a new heart valve, open heart surgery, calls to 911, endless emergency-room visits, and a new cancer growth (that the doctors now wanted to treat with radiation and chemo), Dad said he had had enough. No more hospitals; he was staying home.

Three months later, my dad died peacefully at home in his bedroom and on his own terms. I was fortunate enough to be with him as he took his final breath.

It's been a little over two years since Dad passed away. I feel his presence every day. I try to slow down, stay grounded, keep perspective, and not take anything or anyone for granted. I learned that the most meaningful experiences happen when we are brave enough to be vulnerable about who we are and what we need with the people we love and trust, regardless of the circumstances.

CHAPTER 5

MORE MEDITATIONS

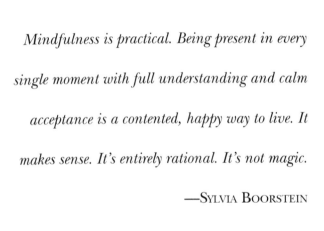

Mindfulness is practical. Being present in every single moment with full understanding and calm acceptance is a contented, happy way to live. It makes sense. It's entirely rational. It's not magic.

—SYLVIA BOORSTEIN

Quiet Sitting Meditation

I f the idea of a more formal meditation feels too daunting or overwhelming, why not simply sit and reflect? Spend a few quiet moments—before doing chores or checking e-mail, before anyone else wakes up—and enjoy some contemplative time in your own private, comfortable space like the couch. One client shared with me that this is her favorite time of day and calls it "The Couch Meditation".

Steps:

1. Find a quiet, comfortable place to sit, like a couch or easy chair. Make sure it's free from distractions, including the phone and TV.

2. Get comfy. You might bring along a cup of coffee or tea and a blanket, if it's chilly, or even invite your favorite pet to join you.

3. Just sit. Treat yourself to a few minutes of quiet time before all of the morning activity.

4. Close your eyes, if you'd like, or keep them open; do whatever feels natural and easy.

5. Reflect, moment by moment. There's no set process or agenda. You might decide to focus on your breath, watch the sunrise, or listen to the birds.

6. Be open to inspiration. As you spend time in reflection, ideas for the day may come to mind. Keep a pen and piece of paper nearby.

7. Sit quietly for five to twenty minutes. When you're ready, stand up, stretch your arms to the ceiling, and start your day, calm and focused.

No matter who you are, you can't sit still all the time. And some people just find it virtually impossible to stay seated and mindful with the levels of pain and agitation and anger they feel. But they can walk with it.

—JON KABAT-ZINN

Walking Meditation

Think of walking as meditation in movement. Taking a walk helps improve mood and calm an overactive, busy mind.

Steps:

1. Make sure you are wearing comfortable shoes.

2. Find a quiet place to walk, preferably in nature.

3. Take a few minutes and begin to focus on your breathing.

4. Once you've spent a few minutes focusing on your breath, start to pay attention to your environment.

5. Decide what you would like to focus on during your walk. Make a commitment to focus on something. Is it the sounds? Is it what you see or what you smell?

6. When you notice your mind wandering, come back to your breath and return to observational mode, reminding yourself of your focus.

7. Continue to walk for ten to fifteen minutes.

There are two ways of spreading light: to be

the candle or the mirror that reflects it.

—EDITH WHARTON, PULITZER PRIZE
–WINNING AMERICAN NOVELIST

Candle Meditation

Why not bring a little light into your meditation? Rather than focus on a mantra, some people find it relaxing, enjoyable, and helpful to gaze at a flame.

Steps:

1. Find a quiet place to meditate.

2. Turn down the lights and close the curtain so your candle will radiate a nice warm glow.

3. Place a lit candle on a table or the ground. You want your candle to be at or slightly below eye level.

4. Take a seat in a comfortable upright position—either on the floor, in a chair, or on the couch.

5. Simply gaze and focus on the flame, allowing any thoughts to gently float away.

6. As you breathe in and out stay focused on the candle, returning your gaze to the flame.

7. As you breathe in, imagine the light gently flowing over your body and warming you. On breathing out, let go of any stress or tension you are holding on to. Repeat.

8. Continue to meditate for five to ten minutes.

Variation 1: Write down one thing you want to let go of on a small piece of paper. It can be anything—a negative thought pattern, a concern, or a challenge. Before you begin the meditation, burn it in the flame. With each breath out, imagine ridding yourself of the thing you want to release.

Variation 2 (for step seven): As you breathe in, imagine the flame starting at the center of your body and slowing spreading across your whole body. As you breathe out, imagine that as you walk through the world, you are sharing your warmth and light with everyone around you.

CHAPTER 6

MORE TOOLS

Mindful Leadership Action Plan

To know and not to do is really not to know.
—Stephen Covey

1. **Benefits:** How will being a more mindful leader benefit me? My colleagues? My family?

2. **Intention and Actions:** In terms of being a more mindful leader, what intention and what actions do I want to set for myself over the next week?

   Examples:

   Intention*: Be present at meetings.*
   Actions*: At meetings I will put my PDA away, turn off my computer, and make eye contact with the person speaking. I will make sure my body language reflects that I am listening.*

   Intention*: Remain calm during difficult moments.*
   Actions*: When I feel things are getting heated during a difficult conversation, I will ask to take a quick coffee break in order to get myself more*

grounded. I will also prepare ahead of time for potentially challenging conversations. I will try the four-step meditation structure "How to Quiet Your Mind in the Midst of Chaos," for ten minutes before work each morning.

Intention*: Listen more and be more open to possibilities.*

Action: *When I am with my team, I will act more as a facilitator and ask for opinions first to encourage others to speak and share ideas. I will wait until others have spoken before I offer my opinion. I will share with my team members that I am working on being a better listener and invite their feedback.*

3. **Learning:** At the end of each day, ask yourself, *What did I notice in terms of "showing up" with intention? What am I prepared to continue to work on? What else might I try?*

Meditation Worksheet

The following worksheet can be used to help support you in your "How to Quiet Your Mind in the Midst of Chaos" meditation or simply as a journal exercise. Either way, it will help you step back, gain perspective, and build reflection into your day.

Step One: Focus on Breath

> *Feelings come and go like clouds in a windy sky. Conscious breathing is my anchor.*
> —THICH NHAT HANH

Notice your state of being by focusing on your breath. What can your breath tell you about how you are feeling?

Examples:
Calm
Grounded
Energized
Agitated
Preoccupied
Tired

_____

_____

_____

_____

Step Two: Have Gratitude

> *Gratitude unlocks the fullness of life. It turns what we have into enough, and more. It turns denial into acceptance, chaos to order, and confusion to clarity. It can turn a meal into a feast, a house into a home, a stranger into a friend.*
> —MELODY BEATTIE

What do you feel grateful for?

Examples:
Abundance
Health
Friendships
Community
Resources
Support

_____

_____

_____

_____

Step Three: Set an Intention

> *Live with intention. Walk to the edge. Listen*
> *Hard. Practice wellness. Play with abandon.*
> *Laugh. Choose with no regret. Appreciate*
> *your friends. Continue to learn. Do what*
> *you love. Live as if this is all there is.*
> —MARY ANNE RADMACHER

How would you like to "show up"? Set your intention for the day.

Examples:
Present
Grounded
Compassionate
Calm during a challenging situation
Objective
Grateful
Joyful
Nonjudgmental
Open to possibilities
Curious

_____

_____

_____

_____

Step Four: Let Go

> *What if we gave up being attached to a certain*
> *outcome and just let it be—not worrying*
> *about how things might or might not turn*
> *out—and lived in the open space of today, this*
> *moment, right now with lightness and joy?*
> —CATHY Q. BAILEY

What are you holding on to that is not serving you? What can you let go of?

Examples:
Need to be liked
Need to be right
To be perfect
Meet others' expectations
Attached to a certain outcome, out of my control
Worrying

_____

_____

_____

_____

Preparing for Difficult Situations

*Give me six hours to chop down
a cherry tree and I will spend the
first four sharpening the axe.*
—ABRAHAM LINCOLN

Many of my clients use the following framework *(thinking through and writing down their thoughts)* before a meeting—in order to strengthen relationships for greater influence and impact to the business.

1. **How do I want to "show up"?** What are the three to five things I would like to hear my colleagues say about me after the meeting? *(e.g., I listened, remained calm, was thoughtful in my responses, and brought a sense of humor to the meeting.)*

2. **What do I want?** What is my goal for this meeting?

3. **What does the other person want?** What does a successful meeting look like from my colleague's point of view?

4. **What is best for the relationship?** What should I say or do in order to further enhance the relationship and lead to more trust?

5. **What is best for the business?** What might I be willing to agree to—or let go of—in the short term in order to achieve greater long-term influence and impact to the business?

6. **How do I minimize drama?** What do I need to refrain from saying that might trigger the other person and make him or her feel defensive?

7. **How do I remain calm?** What could the other person say that might make me feel defensive? How will I prepare myself for the meeting, and what will I do so I don't go into reactive mode? If I do get triggered, how will I get centered again? *(e.g., suggest coffee or bathroom break).*

© Quartner and Associates, LLC 2016

Using an Emotional-Intelligence Framework

IQ gets you hired; EQ gets you promoted

Clients have had success using the following emotional-intelligence framework to self-reflect, self-manage, think about others, and journal. They write down what they're noticing each day and review every week—looking for patterns and trends. The big win in developing emotional-intelligence is stronger leadership presence and improved working relationships.

Self-awareness

1. How is my state of mind *(e.g., relaxed, calm, stressed, etc.)*?

2. What emotions am I experiencing *(e.g., happy, sad, angry, afraid, ashamed, etc.)*?

3. How am I behaving toward myself?

4. How am I behaving toward others?

Self-management

1. What can I do to manage my own emotional state so that I am keeping disruptive emotions and impulses in check *(e.g., meditate, take a deep breath, go for a walk, journal, etc.)*?

2. In this situation, is immediately reacting the best course of action? What might be the benefit of taking time to reflect?

3. How might I best manage my behavior toward others so that it results in a favorable outcome?

Social awareness

1. What am I noticing about the other person's feelings, needs, and experiences?

2. What am I noticing about the other person's body language *(e.g., facial expressions, posture, breathing, tone of voice, etc.)*?

3. What am I doing so that the other person feels like I am engaged with and listening to them *(e.g., making eye contact, leaning toward them, etc.)*?

4. How are my behaviors impacting others around me?

Relationship management

1. What am I doing to contribute to better a relationship with my colleagues *(e.g., collaborating, listening, etc.)?*

2. How am I developing others *(e.g., coaching, mentoring, etc.)?*

3. How am I managing conflict in a way that leads to a successful outcome?

4. How am I leading others? What can I do to inspire my colleagues?

Gratitude Journal

Be thankful for what you have; you'll end up having more. If you concentrate on what you don't have, you will never, ever have enough.
—OPRAH WINFREY

Keeping a gratitude journal helps bring better energy, mood, and perspective to our lives and general overall well-being.

Consider taking a few minutes each night journaling, reflecting on the following questions:

1. What surprised me today?

2. What moved me today?

3. What inspired me today?

A blog entry I shared in 2007 about the value of having gratitude and keeping a gratitude journal...

A Story of Gratitude: How to Be Thankful on Thanksgiving and Not Just About Turkey

Thanksgiving is one of my favorite holidays. We have the opportunity to take a step back and reflect on what we're grateful for and share the day with family and friends. I wrote this story when my father was alive. It continues to stay with me—and I'd like to share it in his memory.

This year is especially meaningful for my family as my father and mother drive to New Jersey to share Thanksgiving with us. We are grateful that my dad is with us, because as he often says, "I'm damn lucky to be here...almost bought the store, and not just once!"

Thankfully, my father's situation has improved and he is on the road to better health as he recovers from aspiration pneumonia and the complications of his illness. Now I watch this man I love find the courage to deal with life on new terms, one where he wears a "trach," uses a feeding tube, and is dependent on oxygen—maybe for the long term but hopefully for the short. He shows gratitude for each new day: a walk around the neighborhood, a good night's sleep, a visit from a friend, or the occasional sip of ice-cold water he sneaks when he thinks no one is watching.

There is amazing power in recognizing what we are grateful for. Recently, a few of my clients have expressed they were stuck in a negative mind-set. We talked about keeping a gratitude journal.

I've learned from the experiences of clients, as well as my own, that writing in a journal helps bring better energy and perspective to our lives. If you feel stuck and are not enjoying life as much as you'd like to, try keeping a gratitude journal, and see what shifts for you. Over time, you will see the impact of how focusing on things you are thankful for has on improving your mind-set and overall well-being.

In addition, we know, based on research, that going into a state of gratitude helps us gain perspective, show up happier, and be more mindful. Mindfulness is the ability to tune into one's self and others and "show up" more centered.

My gratitude journal entry from November 25, 2007:

I was surprised by how much my mother needed my father in her life—any way she could have him. And by my dad's courage to fight for his life, even when it meant putting aside his ego and living in a way he would have never thought he could or would have to.

I was moved by my father's courage and wonderful sense of humor during a challenging time. On many occasions when the nurse showed up with yet another needle, my father jokingly referred to himself as a "human pin cushion." And when one doctor told him he had lung cancer and six months left to live, Dad walked out, laughed, and said, "Don't think I haven't heard that before—if I heard it once, I've heard it a dozen times." Thankfully, the doctor was wrong.

I am inspired to give more to someone in need because I have learned that while I thought I was the one giving, I was really the one receiving.

I am especially grateful to my family, friends, work associates, and clients who supported me during this time so I could give to my dad what he needed and help him get stronger.

Gratitude opens the door to the power, the

wisdom, the creativity of the universe.

—DEEPAK CHOPRA

Closing Summary

Incremental success is better than ambitious
failure...Success feeds on itself.
—TAL BEN-SHAHAR

O ne of the best ways for you to become a more mindful leader and "show up" as your best self is to cultivate a daily reflection practice— whether it's meditation or some other activity like jogging, doing yoga, journaling, or sitting quietly.

You just need to figure out what works best for you. I always tell clients there is no "one size fits all" or "magic pill." So experiment! Try different approaches, tools, and exercises, and then commit to what resonates.

You will find an action plan and additional tools to support you in your journey included in the book and on my website, www.quartner.com.

My hope for you is that after reading this book, you are inspired to cultivate your own "mindfulness" practice and "show up" as your best self.

Favorite Resources

Meditation Experts and Teachers

Jon Kabat-Zinn, PhD

Scientist, writer, and meditation teacher Jon Kabat-Zinn is internationally known for his work in bringing mindfulness practices, especially mindfulness-based stress reduction (MBSR), into the mainstream of medicine and society.

Two of my favorite books by him are *Coming to Our Senses* and *Wherever You Go, There You Are.*

He also has wonderful talks and meditations on YouTube.

Thubten Chodron

Thubten is a Buddhist nun, teacher, and author.

Her approach emphasizes the daily application of Buddhist teachings to our lives.

My favorite book of hers is *Open Heart, Clear Mind.* This book provides a solid overview of Buddha's teachings and how we can apply them to experiencing more peace in our daily lives.

Pema Chödrön

An American Buddhist nun and renowned meditation master, Pema Chödrön provides insights into meditation with focus on compassion and wisdom during difficult times.

My favorite books of hers include *Start Where You Are: A Compassionate Guide to Living* and *The Pocket Pema Chödrön*.

Web Resources

Quartner.com

Offers a variety of meditations and tools in support of Mindful Leadership.

Calm.com

Calm.com is a simple mindfulness-meditation app that brings clarity and peace of mind into your life.

The app offers a free "7 Days of Calm" program, which is a great introduction for beginners.

The app tracks your progress, providing encouraging quotes along your meditation journey.

Headspace

Headspace is a guided meditation app that caters to novice meditators and provides several different meditation sets for building self-esteem, gratitude, and more.

The creator of Headspace wrote a book called *Get Some Headspace* that speaks to busy professionals and how they can incorporate mindfulness into sleep, relationship management, anxiety, self-esteem, gratitude, and more.

MindBodyGreen.com

MindBodyGreen.com is a website and blog whose mission is to revitalize the way people eat, move, and live. With meditations, recipes, and video classes, mindbodygreen (mbg) will help you incorporate mindfulness into all aspects of your mental, physical, and spiritual life.

Mindful.org

Mindful.org offers personal stories, news-you-can-use, practical advice, and insights that provide guidance to corporate managers exploring new ways to cultivate workplace engagement and fulfillment.

ACKNOWLEDGMENTS

Unless someone like you cares a whole awful lot. Nothing is going to get better. It's not.
—DR. SEUSS.

There are many people who supported me in my professional journey and helped make this book a reality—too many to name. I can only acknowledge a few—and do so with deep gratitude and appreciation. Thank you for your wisdom, encouragement, and for caring.

Brad, Ari, and Gabrielle for love, purpose, laughter, family dinners and ski vacations.

My father, mother, brothers, and sister for their love of business and believing anything is possible.

Zinnia Horne for her partnership, generosity of spirit, and enthusiasm for cultivating a meditation practice.

Joan Spindel and Lisa Roberts for everyday phone calls, keeping me grounded in what matters, professional encouragement, and lifelong family friendship.

Amanda Rose, Allison Task, Barry Sagotsky, Beth Filla, David Basch, Jane and Jerry Murphy, Jill Donaldson, Joan Abramowitz, Karen Rubin, Maria Cristina Jimenez,

Maris Jurevis, Nataliya Adelson, Regina Lind, Renee Robertson, Rick Gardner, Scott Gingold, and Scott Kerth for being part of a professional coaching community, opportunities, and friendship over the years.

Amy, Dan and Emily Hoskins, Ido, Ifat, and Ofrey Shatsky, Gila Levin, Neil Wise, and TJC Tichon Ve'od class for the opportunity to bring emerging leadership skills to high-school and college students.

Amy McGowan, Bill Blumberg, Denise Cheskis, Jola Oliver, and Laura Boyd for keeping me grounded in what matters, professional encouragement, and lifelong friendship.

Andrea Joseph and Judy Clare for shared history and lifelong friendship.

Cathy Salerno, Laura Lufrano, Len Bardfeld, Lisa Baryschpolec, Teresita Diaz, Walter Hines, and the rest of J&J team for opportunity, partnership, and critical conversations.

Chicago Booth Ski Team for being part of a fun, professional, and inspirational community.

Christopher Stephen, Dale Moss, Joan Spindel, Joseph Zarge, MD, Len Bardfeld, Meryl Moritz, Rick Gardner,

Sang Lee, Sonya Legg, PhD, and Stephen Parker for generously sharing your personal stories. You have inspired me and countless others to lead more fulfilling careers and lives.

Colleen Bracken, Karen DiNunzio, Lynn Krage, and the rest of the Wharton coaching community for the privilege of being part of the MBA Executive Coaching and Feedback Program and continued professional development opportunities.

Dale Moss for always being there: for writing my very first coaching testimonial, the foreword, sharing his story, and enthusiasm for the book. For being the kind of leader who encouraged me to show up as my best self at British Airways and beyond, really caring, and his continued mentorship and support.

Dana Levitan for early edits to the book, encouragement, and friendship.

Dennis O'Brien, Dominick Volini, Glenn Parker, Margaret Butteriss, Stephen Parker, and Winnie Lanoix for their mentorship, generosity of spirit, and professional opportunities.

Friday and Mitzi for being great officemates and sharing morning walks.

Hazzan Joanna Dulkin and Rabbi Julie Roth for their vision of bringing mindfulness to the Princeton community.

James E. Schrager for personal and professional mentorship starting in business school and continuing throughout my life. For always being there, his entrepreneurial spirit, and support of this book.

Jenifer Wirtshafter for Boost Your Energy, Journey-Fit, and inspiration.

Jill Schwartz for Tuesday meditations, early reading of the book, and friendship.

Larry and Nancy Bailey for treating me like a daughter and their genuine excitement for my business.

Linda Domino, Ayami Yamamichi, Catarina Forys, Kapu Patel, Lisa True, and the rest of Yoga Soul for cultivating friendship, compassion, and mindfulness in our New Jersey community.

Lori Levenson and Bob Lupinacci for early edits, encouragement, and support.

Meryl Moritz for her mentorship, generous spirit, and for always seeing one step ahead of me.

Michael Quanci for bringing the book alive with his creative design.

Mysia Haight, my editor, for her creativity and commitment to excellence.

Natalie Star for her mentorship, being there, and believing this book was possible.

Patti Wold for mindful leadership research, birthday dinners, and yoga.

Rabbi Dr. James Jacobson-Maisels and Rabbi Shapira for inspiration and the meditation "How to Quiet Your Mind in the Midst of Chaos".

Shannon Anderson, and Vincenza Pizzo for their generosity of spirit, embracing mindfulness, and contributing to the book.

Suzanne Keech, my first client, a good and positive person who made the world a better place.

The Jewish Center Community of women for celebration, professional inspiration, and friendship: Abigail Rose, Alexandra Bar-Cohen, Anne Rutman, Cyndi Kleinbart, Debra Bass, Denise Cheskis, Dina Shaw, Ifat Shatsky, Jen Black, Joan Spindel, Karen Rubin, Leslie

Schwartz, Lisa Levine, Nancy Lewis, Nurit Curtiss, Suki Wasserman, Susan Kushner, Tasha Gajewski, and Valerie Stone.

The West Windsor Community of women for celebration, professional inspiration, and friendship: Allison Pastor, Connie Kartoz, Connie Lusdyk, Cyndy Hesterberg, Emily Josephson, Jill Jaclin, Kim Borek, Kim Lowney, Lisa Roberts, Marlene Brown, Nancy Gartenberg, Sonya Legg, and Zhanna Sheykhet.

Tina LeMar of Sheltered Yoga for the privilege and honor of serving.

Wendy Feldman for friendship, professional encouragement, and connecting me to people who made a difference in my life.

And my clients for trusting me with their stories and sharing their wisdom.

About the Author

Cathy Quartner Bailey, president of Quartner and Associates, LLC, works as a leadership coach and workshop facilitator for executive and emerging leaders. Her area of expertise is mindful leadership with focus on leadership presence, communication, conflict management, and emotional-intelligence.

Cathy's style is direct, honest, and supportive. She partners with clients to help them understand the link between leadership and being mindful with focus on "how I show up" versus being stuck in "doing" mode. Her specialties include her 360 interview process, where she works with the client to "hear" the feedback in a respectful and meaningful way as well as helping her clients understand, develop and maintain leadership presence. She offers clients a customized, structured approach to help them achieve their leadership goals by sharing insights, as well as, providing customized tools and assessments.

Cathy has coached and facilitated workshops for executives from Fortune 500 companies and entrepreneurial ventures across a broad range of industries including consumer packaged goods, financial services, food manufacturing, health and beauty, healthcare, insurance, management consulting, music and entertainment, pharmaceutical, technology and internet-related services.

She currently works with Wharton's MBA leadership program as an executive coach and has taught Powerful Tools for Coaching Business Leaders at NYU's Leadership and Human Capital Department.

In addition to her coaching, Cathy offers clients strategic marketing expertise and knowledge of the politics present in organizations based on her experience working at British Airways, Lippincott-Margulies, Warner-Lambert, the Maier Group, and the Federal Reserve Board.

Cathy earned an MBA from the University of Chicago Booth, a certificate in health administration services from the University of Chicago, and a BA from Emory in economics. She is a New York University certified organizational and executive coach.

On a personal note, she enjoys family dinners, walking her dogs, meditation, yoga, and skiing. She lives with her husband, son, daughter, and dogs in the Princeton, New Jersey area.

For more information about Cathy Quartner Bailey's executive coaching services, please visit www.quartner.com or contact her at cqb@quartner.com.

Zinnia Horne

I met Cathy in 2013, when she coached me as part of the Wharton Business School's Executive Coaching and Feedback Program.

We bonded over a mutual interest in mindfulness and the impact it can have on our lives. She was walking proof of the positive effects of meditation on her life and people she coached. I was convinced of the value but had not yet committed to making it a regular practice. After receiving feedback about being emotionally reactive, I was motivated more than ever to try meditation to improve my emotional-intelligence.

While at Wharton, I saw mindfulness become increasingly mainstream. In 2015, a student started the Wharton Mindfulness Club, which now boasts over five hundred members. Across the University of Pennsylvania campus, the belief that mindfulness contributes to developing leaders who are empathetic, grounded, and thoughtful has taken hold. Administration, faculty, and students are collaborating to open avenues to mindfulness for students. The health center offers weekly guided meditations and a mindfulness-based stress-reduction course. People regularly talk about meditation and how it helps them perform better.

We hope that this book provides you with a way to incorporate mindfulness into your personal and professional lives.

Zinnia Horne has worked for a variety of organizations, including Facebook, Google, Upstart Network, and Walmart eCommerce, bringing her expertise in the technology industry, strategy, competitive/data analysis, and entrepreneurship.

She earned an MBA from the University of Pennsylvania Wharton School of Business in marketing and operations and a BS in science, technology, and society from Stanford University. Her honors include Ticketleap Case Competition winner (2014), George Schirer Merit Fellowship recipient (2013, 2014), and Google Founder's Award recipient (2011).

She began meditating as a way to enhance her relationships and was hooked when she realized the ripple effects on all aspects of her life. Zinnia is passionate about health, science, and technology and is a proud foodie.

SHELTERED YOGA

T en percent of royalties from *Show Up as Your Best Self: Mindful Leaders, Meditation, and More* will be donated to Sheltered Yoga.

Sheltered Yoga is a nonprofit organization that provides evidence-based, trauma-informed, mental and behavioral health and wellness curriculum through yoga, meditation, and mindfulness. Serving individuals in homeless and women's shelters, depressed and alternative schools, prisons, outreach programs, foster programs, and recently homeless residential communities, it aims to increase self-esteem, self-worth, self-compassion, and tolerance.

Sheltered Yoga's vision is to work hand in hand with facilities and communities across the nation to not only bring about a positive change in each individual it serves but also create a positive movement. As individuals become more empowered, focused, and hopeful, they affect their families in a positive way, and the families affect their communities in which they live in a positive way.

Sheltered Yoga's motto is bringing a "can do" attitude to people in need.

For more information, please visit www.shelteredyoga.org.

"Practice sharing the fullness of your being,

your best self, your enthusiasm, your vitality,

your spirit, your trust, your openness, above

all, your presence. Share it with yourself,

with your family, with the world."

—JON KABAT-ZINN

28437331R10102

Made in the USA
Columbia, SC
18 October 2018